CW00342894

FLORA SOAMES · THE ONE DAY BOX

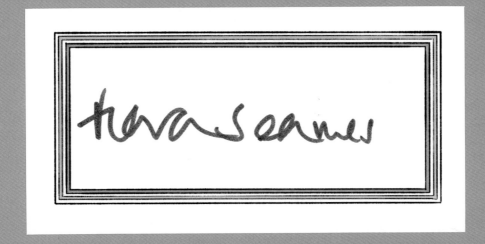

*This book is written in memory
of both my grandmothers, whose style
and spirit set me on my way, and
Ant Gordon Lennox, whose belief
in me, and in the creativity
of so many, was the catalyst
for so much.*

*This book is dedicated to my parents
and the home they have created.
And to Blondie — the very best find of all.*

FLORA SOAMES

THE ONE DAY BOX

A Life-Changing
Love of Home

RIZZOLI
NEW YORK

New York Paris London Milan

Introduction

T HIS IS A STORY ABOUT MY OUT-OF-control collecting habit. It is also a scrapbook about where that obsession has led me, and a love letter to the role that home has played in my life.

I have always treasured things, specifically the collecting and arranging of objects that evoke a strong feeling of home. The One Day Box is the embodiment of that passion: growing up, leaving home and latterly becoming an interior designer, it has increasingly defined how I live and the work that I do.

The label itself derived from a great friend. About ten years ago, I shared some of what I'd collected with him to show off a torn roll of wallpaper I was excited about. As I teetered on a ladder leaning against my cupboard, struggling to find what I was looking for from a box stuffed with random things, he questioned the purpose of these disparate items. While I talked about the irresistible alchemy of nostalgia and inspiration that every piece represented, trying desperately to sound like a collector and not a hoarder, he kindly called it my One Day Box. I felt an immediate gratitude to him for validating my eccentric, wildly fantastical, and more than slightly extravagant hobby, and the name stuck.

My definition of a One Day Box is a place, real or imaginary, where we store fragments of our past that spark a feeling of connection – memories of sights, smells and sounds we love, and to which one day we hope to return. For me, what started in a shoebox soon graduated into a trunk, and before long lined the shelves of a shed. It was a collection of a myriad of things that appealed to me, from textiles and fragments of wallpaper to pieces of furniture, glassware and lamps, but also photographs, letters and much that I just could not bear to throw away. All of them are precious for different reasons, but together they create a patchwork of associations that reflect my concept of home.

I consider every object in my One Day Box to be a thing of great beauty, not just because of their aesthetic qualities but also because of the feelings they evoke. They all spark a sense of self that I find simultaneously grounding and uplifting, no matter what is going on in my life. Each item has anchored me as much as it has propelled me forward.

Many of us have an equivalent – whether tucked away in the recesses of our imagination and memory or close to hand in a battered folder. A large part of what fascinates me about my job as an interior decorator is getting the chance to discover other people's collections. It is a great privilege to explore with my clients why they have a strong attraction to certain objects and designs. I consider much of my role to be about carrying their One Day Box with them and finding ways to bring it to life in their home.

Our One Day Boxes change as we change. Things that mean something at one time can resonate quite differently at another. Our relationship with the people and places around us is constantly evolving, and our notion of home does much the same. But the places where I feel most at home are those where life – friends and family, from the past and the present – takes centre stage. In this book I hope to celebrate the human experience that lies therein.

CHAPTER ONE

Home and

Heritage

LIKE MOST PEOPLE, I MOVED A COUPLE OF times in my childhood, but my idea of home is in every respect singular. When I think of home, no other place features. This house belongs to my parents and has been the single most formative influence on me, not just in how I go about my work, but how I go about my life, too.

My memory of home is visceral. It is the view from a particular step when something especially important happened. It's the smell and the light and the open door that my siblings and I were too scared to go past at night. It is the place that I miss, still, and the place where I felt safe enough to try on different versions of myself. It's not a particular colour of paint on the chart that I remember, but the feeling that the colour inspired in me. It's the sound of my father shuffling newspapers in his armchair, the smell of my mother's scent, the promise of life leaving us alone just for a bit to indulge in whatever fantasy was at play. It was everything except what a brochure would tell you. For me, home isn't bricks and mortar, it is feelings.

As you would expect given what I do, I've spent a fair amount of time thinking about and discussing different interpretations of home and what people want from their own. Everyone's lives and styles are different, but everyone wants a place that supports and elevates the daily process of living. And if that is truly the aim, who cares if it looks great if it doesn't feel fabulous? A home isn't about being an emblem of what someone has achieved; it is about how you want to feel and de facto who you are and what matters to you. For me, that's an infinitely more interesting objective.

Formally known as a library, this room is the amalgamation of fabrics new and old – a vintage Colefax and Fowler Eugenie chintz armchair sits alongside a well-travelled lacquered trunk from Hong Kong. The bougainvillea is kept company by a painting of a French villa by my great-grandfather.

What's gone before

For most of my childhood, I was brought up with my sister, Gemma, and my brother, Archie, at our parents' home in North Norfolk, where they still live today. My mother inherited the house from her parents and grew up there herself. She knew nowhere else. An Edwardian house built by my great-grandfather and very much of its time, its entire *modus operandi* has always been about comfort over aesthetics, made evident the minute you cross the threshold.

At the heart of the house is a galleried hall that means you always have a sense of where everyone is and what they're doing. It connects each space seamlessly to the rooms around it, and with that, the people in them. My siblings and I were often caught past our bedtime sticking our heads through the bannisters to spy on the action below. For me, this house, and specifically how my mother felt about it and nurtured it, infuses everything I feel about the concept of home.

Taking on the house and its working farm was a significant responsibility for my parents. Having grown up there, my mother knew that she had an important role to play in preserving and protecting a way of life, as well as giving back to the community. As a place she loved deeply, she understood what it took to keep the story going, which she did wholeheartedly. We have all been aware, for as long as I can remember, of what a privilege and joy it was to grow up there.

My mother poured huge effort and energy into the upkeep of the house and its decoration, as well as the garden and its design, but she did so in a way that never seemed self-conscious or contrived. Yes,

right
My mother surrounded
by dogs, an impressive six
here. The deep red baize
curtains give a richness
and depth to a room
littered with texture and
pattern. A commissioned
ikat-covered modern
ottoman is weighed down
by objects and the Dahlias
lampshades and cushions,
all at a jaunty angle, add
to the air of informality.

following pages
An overflowing
breakfront bookcase
dominates the library
wall and says so much
about how my mother
presents the things she
loves. Volumes of books
(historical and otherwise),
Christmas cards from
years gone by, a pair of
needlework bellpulls
which I recently gave her
to hang just here, 1970s
Murano glass vases, a bust
of my great-grandmother
and a plethora of friendly
faces litter the shelves.

The galleried hall is the central room from which everything else extends. As an interior its proportions lend themselves to large-scale works of art, immense furniture and memorable gatherings. The walls were painted in the 1950s by the specialist decorator Jim Smart, and give a warm backdrop to more robust colours and textures in various fabrics. A generous drinks table greets you as you reach the bottom of the stairs and a patchwork of antique carpets map out the wooden floorboards.

A vast arrangement of flowers from the garden always sits on the piano, from cotinus and cardoons in the late summer months, to cherry blossoms in the spring and clematis and hawthorn berries in the winter months. Their seemingly thrown together appearance is typical of my mother's way of living with flowers.

above

A magnificent plaster horse's head, rescued by my mother from the floor of an antique shop in Arezzo, sits in pride of place surrounded by albums and books – a constantly shifting display of my parents' hobbies and interests. The overmantle mirror has always hung in this position, and I recently sourced the gilded Italian wall lights to frame it on this immense wall.

there was planning, but things weren't over-thought, and the experience was not translated as an arduous process. It was about inspiring continuity, inclusivity and appreciation, rather than anything imposed.

My mother and I have always enjoyed detailed conversations about interiors, objects and collecting. It is a language and a passion that we share. I can't remember it being otherwise, and I love that it continues today. Her deep-rooted connection to her home, her belief that it was special because of the many people who loved it, and her sense that we should all live in it with respect but not reverence, all stayed with me. She was not afraid to make mistakes and we spent hours together reimagining rooms and rearranging furniture, as we still do today. For her, expressing herself in her surroundings is about people and celebration. It has always been fun.

Within all of this, I have inherited her love of the things that tell a story about your life, however insignificant they might seem to others. The moth-eared, hugging koalas that someone gave her mother which now sit on her own bedroom chest of drawers and have done for fifty years are one of her most treasured belongings. It's not just that a

right

A portrait of my mother's grandfather in his 7th Hussars full dress uniform watches over the landing, offset by a pair of 19th-century French linen curtains I stumbled across in a local shop twenty years ago, made to fit this large window with now sun-faded velvet leading edges. A buddha collected on my mother's travels to Burma in the 1980s peers out from the windowsill.

left
On a typically wet day in August, my mother watches over the Hunter rose that her father planted sixty years ago.

above
A natural and passionate gardener, my mother's flower room is as important as any other room in the house where perovskia and buddleia spill over the worktop and, whatever the weather, the outside is brought inside.

thing sparks some kind of aesthetic pleasure, it's that it also triggers a memory – of the person who gave it, or the moment it was found, and the thoughts it inspires.

The specific hue of the blue on the walls in my parents' bedroom is just a backdrop to the conversations we shared curled up on the end of their bed. The blousiness of the floral print of her curtains sets an informal tone that made me feel safe when I tiptoed through the door as a child. This room is the ultimate expression of the informal beauty of my mother's style.

As an extension of this, and part of the same approach, my mother is a great present giver. She chooses things that are intended for keeping. Every birthday and Christmas she gave us something that she'd found and loved, and knew we would cherish. They weren't lavish, and I wasn't always at an age to appreciate them at the time, but there isn't a chipped teacup, small drawing or piece of dachshund paraphernalia she's given me that doesn't now have pride of place in my own home.

following pages
Originally a myriad of corridors and storage rooms, this boot room was opened up to accommodate the overflowing collection of muddy clothing, a permanent feature of this house. A billiards room that connects off these rooms at the back of the house is home to the clothes of my ancestors. My grandfather's Scots Guards forage caps and bowler hats are housed here (and often worn for fancy dress).

LOCK & C?
HATTERS,
St James's Street,
LONDON.

REGISTERED TRADE MARK

previous pages
The house revolves
around a central
courtyard, onto which
the cloakroom loos face.
Edwardian sinks stand
proud with hand-painted
tiles, and an overhanging
embroidered Turkish
fragment is converted
into a blind. Memorabilia
spanning the years
document the fusion of
families throughout the
generations.

left
My parents' bedroom
is a treasure trove of
things collected – frayed
cushions, portraits of
myself, my grandmother
and her brother, all as
young children. This
gentle but evocative floral
print envelops the room
with Enid, my fourteen-
year-old dachshund,
sunbathing as is her
usual custom.

following pages
Trinkets collected from
my mother's travels
hang on a bureau. A
photograph of me with
my father is tucked
behind a gilded oak-leaf
mirror that I have always
coveted; a photograph of
my grandmother in pink
sits alongside the quilted
cotton and ticking-lined
bed tester; soft voile
curtains frame an aged
dressing table, used as
much to display everyday
items as anything else.

A legacy shared

opposite
Assorted blue and white plates collected over the years are staggered on an end kitchen wall looking through the pantry toward a more formal panelled dining room beyond.
A portrait of much-loved dogs drawn by my aunt sits above the opening.

Decorating a house is not a language my father has engaged in greatly; how a home makes you feel, however, is another matter. His mother tongue is the welcoming and including of others, ideally enjoying something delicious. He is a passionate cook and we love discussing recipes, cooking and eating together. In my mind's eye, my father is at the centre of the kitchen, absorbing the life around him. He has always had a gentle and understanding presence – evidenced by the fact that my friends often seek him out for his company and counsel, as do we all.

He comes from a large family, one defined by noisy coming-togethers, played out around the table, full of affection for each other and demonstrative displays of love. It's not unusual for them to cry when they see each other – in fact it is encouraged. They have endless terms of endearment designed to support and envelop each other, to 'put out a paw' or exclaim 'wow' down the telephone as a kind of verbal hug, a phrase inherited from their grandfather, Winston Churchill when he signed off to his wife, Clementine. We have all benefited from the legacy of that emotional inheritance.

In marrying my mother, my father's approach to life fit with ease into her family home. His charm and informality complement her own, and though he didn't get bogged down in the menial detail of life, he was the greatest cheerleader of our every day. My father's extraordinary heritage and upbringing littered the walls and shelves around us. That expression is as much about love for those personalities as it about sharing a legacy, something he has always taken seriously but worn lightly. There's a nonchalance to my parents' approach which I admire and the story of what they have created at home is very much a shared one.

following pages
Once a series of rooms, this kitchen was created to become the heart of everything. A pediment frames the aga with Delft tiles, and an oversized bronzed oak-leaf chandelier hangs above the island. The sofa breaks up the room between cooking and eating, covered in Cornucopia cushions, old blankets and yet more dogs.

My father catching up on the daily news in the place he can so often be found. Chevron-patterned upholstered dining chairs line a refectory table and soft urn-printed curtains frame french doors onto the kitchen garden.

Opposite is a portrait of his grandparents, accompanied by him as a young boy aged seven in shorts and a tie, his brother and elder sister, all arriving at the christening of their youngest brother Rupert, at the Royal Hospital, Chelsea.

previous pages
The dresser in the kitchen
is a landscape of all of our
lives. My mother's love
for collecting is in full
flight, a myriad of objects
is used to prop up cards
collected and photographs
of those we love. Feathers
are stored like pens in a
pot, the telephone and
Noah's Ark sit side by
side and quite literally a
wallpaper of faces and
the happiest of moments
are the backdrop to this
evolving scene.

The fridge door and the dresser in the kitchen are the ultimate expression of my parents' ethos. The photographs, certificates, clippings cut out from the newspaper, decades-old birthday cards and handwritten notes are the wallpaper of our family life. A bird's nest that has fallen from a tree in the garden is cherished on the top shelf, alongside a love heart scrawled by a grandchild and an Elvis mug to commemorate my father's annual Heartbreak Hotel performance. It is a shrine to what they care about most – the two and four legged friends and family who make them happy and the moments that go hand in hand with this. It is their definition of the highest form of love and praise: if you end up on the fridge door, you have quite literally made it.

above
The display of photographs
in a haphazard manner
has become a family
tradition. Weddings, formal
portraits and moments in
time jostle for attention
on this ox-blood gloss
corridor wall.

right
A lacquered Buddha
and a Nanking charger
sit alongside a photo
of my first dachshund,
Squirvy, an image of my
great-grandmother Maudie,
a cut-out of my grandfather
and a postcard of my
great-grandfather on a
naval voyage.

right
The pulling together of this room was something that I was integrally involved in and the inclusion of my mother and my shared favourite palette of aubergine and soft greens is championed here. A spectacular collection of porcelain hangs around a landscape of an olive grove, which would otherwise be far too small for this prominent position. A large print sits on the sofa alongside more decadent weaves and textured velvets surrounding the mantelpiece.

following pages
I encouraged my mother to drag these pelmets, originally from a previous home, out from the depths of a dusty store and re-hang them with this opulent looking but simple inexpensive stripe. As avid card players, members of our family often occupy these chairs. The faded antique bridge cloth was one of the better presents I have given my mother.

The out-of-control plumbago planted by my grandmother smothers the furniture around it in this small glasshouse, while the leaking panes above don't hinder sunny drinks in this room.

CHAPTER TWO

A

Pat. 7919

Habit Inherited

Top shelf (books, left to right):

THE PLACES IN BETWEEN — RORY STEWART

Beautiful Ruins — Jess Walter

THE WILD OTHER — NANCY MITFORD — CLOVER STROUD

JOSEPHINE TEY — Miss Pym Disposes

Educated: A Memoir — TARA WESTOVER

Daphne du Maurier — DON'T LOOK NOW

The Visit of the Royal Physician

Alex Soojung-Kim Pang

MACKENZIE — Whisky Galore

The Kite Runner — Khaled Hosseini

ALEXANDRA LAPIERRE

Caught by the River: A COLLECTION OF WORDS ON WATER

Bottom shelf (books, left to right):

Emotional — The Piano Tuner — DANIEL MASON — DANIEL GOLEMAN

VASARI · LIVES OF THE ARTISTS VOLUME I

Chinua Achebe — Things Fall Apart

Dangerous Muse: A LIFE OF CAROLINE BLACKWOOD — NANCY SCHOENBERGER

DODIE SMITH — I CAPTURE THE CASTLE

THICH NHAT HANH — THE ART OF LIVING

The Art of Hearing Heartbeats — JAN-PHILIPP SENDKER

ER of the PARTY — Polygon

LARSSON — The Girl with the Dragon Tattoo — Quercus

The Secret Scripture — SEBASTIAN BARRY

DIANA ATHILL — Instead of a Book: Letters to a Friend — GRANTA

FROM THE AGE OF ABOUT ELEVEN, I COULD not not stop collecting things. It was compulsive and felt like an extension of myself, but it was a hobby I admitted to few.

As I grew older, my collecting habit gathered momentum. I'm not talking about an intellectual or commercial endeavour that is connected in any way to status. I am talking about amassing things that spark an irresistible emotional response: the searching for, the finding of and the hanging on to things to which I felt a visceral connection. I have not and have never been a specialist in what I collect. I am in every which way a magpie.

I am the first person to say that there is a very thin line between something 'collected' and something clung on to for dear life. The fact that I still have my dachshund Enid's whiskers in a pot on my mantelpiece from fifteen years ago probably tells you all you need to know. There is something superstitious and deeply sentimental in my approach, perhaps a desire to hold on to my past, or at least things that remind me of people from the past, in the face of change. I like to think of it as a stabilising influence, my collecting habit has always kept me company and held my hand.

Ways of seeing

below
An old Afghani scarf pulled out of the dressing-up chest sits alongside my grandmother's photo album showing pages of my sister and cousin, gallivanting around on her floral-printed swing seat, and the surrounding garden resplendent with azaleas.

I am particularly fascinated by what drives others to collect, and can pick out fellow-hoarders at a crowded car boot sale. Both of my grandmothers celebrated this approach to collecting with me while I was growing up and had a formative impact on my style. Their confidence in what they collected, consciously or otherwise, and how they put these things together, kindled my own desire to do the same. Their enjoyment in the process of bringing life to their surroundings was something to which I aspired: not to display things the done way; quite the opposite. They celebrated their love of something by the simple act of putting it on a mantelpiece. That is the source of my fascination with collecting and was the beginning of my own One Day Box.

right
The tradition of black-and-white photographs 'en masse' continues on my cloakroom wall, with many of the same images my mother has at home reappearing again.

I WINSTON SPENCER CHURCHILL
M.P. C.H. CHANCELLOR of the
UNIVERSITY of BRISTOL
DECLARE THERE to be NO
FINER HOSTEL THAN
WILLS HALL AMONG
THE UNIVERSITIES of
the BRITISH EMPIRE

Dama

My grandmother on my mother's side, Dama, was a collector of stuff extraordinaire. She would tell vivid stories of her childhood through her explanation of the things that decorated her home in Norfolk, which she continued to fill with unbridled enthusiasm throughout her life.

Her childhood was marked with sadness. Both of her adored brothers died young, at the end of and shortly after the Second World War respectively, leaving her family bereft. Displaying things that reminded her of them was a life-force for her. She kept her childhood within reach at all times, constantly telling us stories about her beautiful young brothers, celebrating her family wherever she could. Even as a child I could sense that she was holding on tightly to what had gone before, with no intention of letting go.

To me, her passion in life seemed to be the pursuit of the beautiful and the eclectic, often sourced from local dealers, all of whom became her best friends. She loved the act of shopping, in particular the hunt

left and above
My grandmother standing with her one-eyed dachshund, Phoebe, and another portrait, glamorous as ever with scarlet lips and nails, taken with my mother aged three.

Swaebe

for a bargain, which to her was akin to panning for gold. Her collecting was manic and she revelled in that identity too, with me as her adoring sidekick, beady eyes and empty bags at the ready. Whether trailing the local car boot sale, charity shop or high street, that's what we did and that's what we enjoyed together.

It wasn't just the shopping but also the act of arranging and displaying her trove that gave her such pleasure. She was constantly plumping cushions and making what felt like a performance of the whole thing. Everything was colour co-ordinated, matchy matchy to the extreme. She amassed huge collections of china that blended in with the walls, the curtains, the tiebacks and even the books that lined the shelves. There was pink tissue paper to match the pink sink and the pink carpet. Her bedroom was an explosion of powder blue, from the bed covers to the dressing table to her bed jacket. Even her rattan pully basket, known as Betty, which she took with her to the market every Thursday, had bespoke covers made for it to match her outfits. Staying with Dama was heaven, with my cousins, siblings and me being allowed not just to pile into her bed with her but to sleep there too, all of us enveloped in threadbare sheets surrounded by countless crocheted cushions and her three adored dachshunds.

She was beautiful and glamorous and always immaculately put together. Everything was fastidiously stored away, from belts to lipsticks to dresses that she kept for us. She prefaced everything by saying, 'this will be yours one day', perhaps referring to a pair of worn bedside slippers or some lace she had stumbled across, which she offered up to my sister and me for our wedding veils when we were just five and seven.

Dama's collecting was an extension of herself – colourful, full-hearted and all-encompassing. She derived huge pleasure from involving others, all of whom adored her for her inclusive and generous spirit and for taking them with her on her journey to the past. She was adept at making life fun for those around her, especially in the way she created a home and talked about that process. She didn't follow rules and we loved her for it.

A timeless photograph of my grandmother aged eighteen, one year before marrying my grandfather, shows her dressed for a ball wearing black – everyone else wore white. It sits on top of a backdrop of her own collected and now frayed rosettes.

For each of her grand-
children, Dama collected
postcards of a specific
flower. Mine was Lily
of the Valley, my sister's
Forget me Nots. These
lovingly collected and
compiled albums, bought
from market stalls and
newsagents spanning
the years, with the pages
still smelling as they did
when I poured over them
as a young girl, are the
ultimate expression of
her love of collecting
and her love for her
grandchildren, as well as
being emblematic of the
aesthetic of her childhood.
   My card table, which
was once hers, sits in the
corner of my sitting room
today, with her signature
fuchsia pink velvet cloth
on top.

Grandmama

My grandmother on my father's side was Mary Soames, the youngest daughter of Winston and Clementine Churchill. She was graceful, charming, compassionate and an extraordinary force. She was a brilliant writer and orator, and a prolific author. Much of her life was dedicated to the legacy of her parents and the life she lived at their side.

The family home, creating one and welcoming others into it, mattered deeply to her. Her childhood was spent at Chartwell in Kent, against the backdrop of her father's political career. She was acutely aware of her role as her parents' child of consolation, born after their daughter Marigold had died aged two. The youngest of four siblings by many years, she brought joy, amusement, solace and companionship to her parents throughout their lives.

Her mother, my great-grandmother, Clemmie Churchill, was adept at making a home that welcomed visitors into the warmth and energy of family life. Statesmen and colossal personalities came together

below
A well-known image of my grandmother's father, but perhaps less so of my grandmother. Here she is seen accompanying her father when he received the Freedom of the City of London in June 1943.

left
Poised to tell a joke mid-cigar, my grandmother was a fantastic raconteur.

above
The library at
Chartwell as it still
stands today with
its floral chintz of
chrysanthemums, not
unlike my Dahlias print
in feel. The bookcases
house a model of
Mulberry Harbour at
Port Arromanches,
given to my great
grandfather as a record
of the planning of the
D-Day landings.

there, with everyone included around the dining room table. From
Charlie Chaplin to Lawrence of Arabia and President Truman, my
grandmother was often included in these gatherings where it was first
and foremost a family home – for those who lived there and those
who visited.

Chartwell is a deeply sensory place and can be visited today as a
museum where their family life is lovingly documented. The smell
of Winston's cigars still lingers in the wood panelling in the hall, not
unlike a humidor. Both the richness of the colours in the library, where
a vibrant floral print springs out amidst the more masculine book-lined
shelves, and an armchair that gives you a warm hug in an otherwise
quite austere setting, carry the personalities of both my great-grandmother and great-grandfather in tandem.

As a result of her upbringing, my grandmother was defined by
family and the family home. At the centre of almost all of her adult
life was her husband, Christopher, and their five children. As a dip-
lomat's wife she was always finding the balance between public life

right
My grandmother's
trunk is filled with
letters, diaries and
documents. Tablecloths
she made and stored live
to tell the tale of another
party. Telegrams, lists
of names that chart
significant moments in
her and her family's life
and the album recording
the decoration of
her own home, all
sit scattered over her
Portuguese needlework
rose-strewn rug in my
now study.

left

My grandmother and grandfather walking in the garden at the British Residence in Paris, with those timeless striped awnings and the elegant glazed gallery beyond. As well as a gardening diary, my grandmother kept seed packets, shown here as a backdrop, spanning decades, documenting the many gardens she planted.

and entertaining, and their private life. Holding this all, and being at the heart of both, was the drumbeat of her every day. For her, family always came first.

The British Residence in Paris, where during the late 1960s my grandfather was Ambassador, had a fabled sitting room named the Salon Vert. My grandmother made it her own the moment they arrived, just by living in it. It remained formal, with inherited seating that was uncharacteristically upright for her style. Despite that, the room took on a new lease of life, distinct from anything that had gone before, in the way that the space was inhabited by them all. It was there that they came together as a family, her teenage children lounging on chairs, Jim the pug lying in front of the fire, Romeo and Juliet, the pair of doves, cooing at each other in the corner of the room, and a resident mouse who would make his journey along the top of the gilded dado rail to eat the birdseed while no one was looking. When I ask those who visited the residence during that time about what they remember the most, they instantly recount what it made them feel – a deep sense of home.

below

A born archivist, this is my grandmother's recording of the details of a Christmas party thrown at the British Residence alongside a letter she sent me – I've tried to take a leaf out of her book by keeping them all.

My grandmother's home towards the end of her life was in a quiet street in West London. Crammed with her favourite things, it was a visual and celebratory tapestry of an interesting life lived.

In the leafy streets of Holland Park, West House was like visiting a country cottage in London, approached by a winding path. She knew exactly what she wanted in the way of interiors and enlisted the help of Dinah Marriott to implement colours and patterns in styles that were evocative of previous homes she had lived in.

Despite appearances, as with her parents, my grandmother made frugal and canny design decisions in her own home. She knew exactly what she wanted and it was not about aspiring to grandeur. It was a quality she inherited from her mother, for whom balancing the books with Winston's whims and expensive taste, was a continual tightrope. She was nostalgic and sentimental, treasuring and enjoying her belongings, while documenting the story of her past, a task she achieved to great effect. She had a keen eye for detail and diarised the everyday. Every letter received or sent and every receipt was filed away, every recipe tried in her kitchen was stored in a box, and every seed planted in her garden was noted in her book. She was a repository for the life that she lived, as well as for the legacy that she carried with her.

During my twenties, my flat in London was a few streets away from West House, where Grandmama lived towards the end of her life. I would visit regularly. She was involved, interested and always interesting, often with a bottle of Pol Roger on the go, especially of an evening when I would curl up on the sofa to watch a film with her. She was enormously encouraging of my work, and constantly noticed and celebrated the effort that went into making a space feel a certain way. When she wanted me to restore a pair of worn fireside chairs, her specific request was that everything should remain the same – the Bennison print, the studs, the hue – but most importantly, their comfort. I couldn't have agreed with her more.

West House was like a time capsule: everything in it was exceptional, whether because of its provenance or simply by dint of her having chosen it. Her father's red leather dispatch box sat by the front door and was used to contain dog-poo bags to be grabbed when heading out with Plum for a walk. That lightness of touch and complete lack of pomposity defined everything she did. She was the maypole around which we all danced and the matriarch we adored, and her home was an extension of that.

She placed much importance on the positioning of books and paintings throughout. Works by Oscar Nemon, John Lavery, William Nicholson, as well as the paintings of her father, an amateur but accomplished artist, took pride of place alongside objects gathered on her travels. They were the things she grew up with, and those she collected with my grandfather throughout their lives, and were much loved by dint of the personalities and moments in time they carried with them.

Seemingly cluttered, but with everything having its place, it was a house to be shared with us all, and those memories are long-lasting as a result.

An urge to collect

below
The beginnings of
a damask collection
starting to take
shape, always colour
co-ordinated but rarely
so neatly stored away.

This emerging narrative about the amassing of objects with significance meant that as I started to move around in my teenage years, I would carry a startling amount of stuff with me. The packing and unpacking of my suitcase was a ritual, going way beyond having enough socks to get through the week. This travelling circus approach, the complete opposite to travelling light, stayed with me when I moved away to university, later when I worked in Italy and when I returned to London in my twenties. I was emphatic about decorating every inch of my walls wherever I went, whether it would be my home for weeks, months or years. Photos, postcards and random bits of fabric were the things that grounded me, and creating an environment that was my own became my safety net. Friends would visit and stay, and for

right
Needlepoint pieces
amassing over time,
every one of them with
its own story to tell.

some it was probably too much. But for others in search of respite, it was a momentary sanctuary from where they could then go out and be normal again.

I was drawn to working with beautiful things and after a short stint in the art world I ended up with a role at a furniture emporium in London – a place where I felt at home. Learning from someone with an extraordinary and deeply eclectic vision, my eyes were opened to the professional world of collecting and dealing, and the compelling stories and characters involved. The experience gradually began to give reason to my collecting habit being more than just a serious amount of clobber, and they were formative years.

My transition into the world of interior design was an entirely organic one. Conversations I was having with people about the objects they were buying very naturally morphed into discussions about how these would come together in their own homes. I didn't have any professional training, nor did I have a portfolio of work to showcase my style, but I did have an eye, which I was developing along the way, and an enthusiasm to put this into practice. I remain enormously grateful to those early clients who, in choosing me, took a huge leap of faith and set me on my path.

All the while I continued to collect, for goodness knows what or where. It satiated a mix of curiosity, nostalgia and a need to express myself, as others might do through words or painting. There was always something ritualistic and deeply soulful about the process for me. A bedspread from a stall in L'Isle-sur-la-Sorgue while on holiday; a decanter and glasses from a dusty shop in North Yorkshire; a cracked plate from every time I visited my favourite porcelain dealer in Norfolk. It seemed random, and there was no apparent end goal, but gradually, disparate transactions took on a shared personality: a collection of things I was compelled to take home.

My love for, but little knowledge of, glassware started shortly after my hoarding of fabrics. Well-travelled, much-used and often kept in this handsome Arts and Crafts cabinet, I find their jewel-like quality irresistible.

right
Like everything, my collection of china is driven by magpie tendencies. Lustreware, Creamware, Aptware and gleaming Fornasetti plates, to name a few, a lot of my collection is chipped but each and every piece is very much treasured.

following pages
A collection of Sunderland Lustreware, with its romantic connotations in imagery and its distinctive palette, combined with its simplicity of design, stands proud on an intricate chinoiserie cabinet, with a 19th-century French Indienne wallpapered screen as its backdrop, in my home.

THE SAILORS FAREWELL
Far from home across the sea,
To foriegn climes I go,
While far away O think of me,
And I'll remember you.

NORTHUMBERLAND 74.

CHAPTER THREE

Sense of Place

Sense of Self

I WAS LIVING AND WORKING IN LONDON and finding my feet as an interior decorator when I met an extraordinary man – Ant. I was in my twenties, feeling at times a bit untethered, but when I got together with him, I felt immediately understood.

Our time together involved various comings and goings, with a peripatetic existence and busy working lives, but our relationship was heartfelt and life-changing. Though he didn't share my obsession for home-making, he was intrigued by it, constantly celebrating what I did. Ant believed wholeheartedly in authenticity, a creed he followed religiously. He had a way with people, compounded by his intuition and the disarming stories he told about his own life. We were amused by each other's dysfunctionalities, and our shared life celebrated the unusual and eccentric. Our meeting set me on a course that would shape me to the core.

A love lived

In the autumn of 2017, after eight years together, Ant died after a short illness.

Soon after his funeral it became clear to me that I needed to return to Ant's home near the Norfolk coast, where we had spent so much time together. Everyone behaves differently in grief. For me at that stage, I needed to immerse myself fully in his cottage, staring at the sharp end and living the otherwise unbelievable reality that he wasn't there any more. What I didn't know at the time was that the brutality of those first steps was a vital part of being able to take the steps that would follow.

I was compelled to play out the patterns of our life when we were together: the walks we went on; the food we kept in the fridge; the music we listened to; the programmes we watched. The bedtime routine of running a bath, my clothes on my chair, turning his light out last at night. Those daily rituals that make up the way we live, on which we hinge so much of our happiness without knowing it. As the days passed, my dependence on the things that represented our life together felt like clinging to a raft in a deep and dark sea. My relationship with those things – his things, my things and our things sitting alongside each other – was a vital part of those days too.

Unimaginable change had been forced upon me and there was no doubt that further change lay ahead. I had to charge myself to comprehend moving away from this home, and to understand what I needed as a space in which to grieve on the other side.

When the time came to leave the cottage, I had no more to give and was utterly depleted. My family and friends were extraordinary and their overwhelming support was ever-present. But being in their homes made me feel exposed and I knew that in creating my next place to be, I needed to shift my focus on to designing an environment that would hold me in my grief.

That's when the Pheasantry came into my life.

The cottage in the woods

left
The winding drive to
the Pheasantry on a
winter's morning, the
expansive parkland with
its magnificent trees
shown to great effect in
the cold January light.

The Pheasantry is an old keeper's cottage on the borders of North Dorset and Wiltshire. It is small and perfectly formed, with a symmetrical façade and a curiously mismatched back end. Made of local greenstone of a dark grey colour, it is reached by a winding drive and surrounded on three sides by rambling woods. As winter starts to peter out, carpets of snowdrops cover the woodland floor as far as you can see, replaced by bluebells and wild garlic at the arrival of spring. The views out of the front of the cottage are of sweeping parkland with open, rolling hills beyond. It is simultaneously cosy and spectacular, isolated and welcoming. It is entirely complete in and of itself.

Though moving to Dorset felt as if I was putting a pin in a map of uncertainty, I was drawn here because it wasn't entirely new to me. Ant and I had spent much time here with the closest of friends, and when they suggested taking on the lease for this cottage, it immediately felt like the right thing to do. It was a great source of comfort to return to a place that was familiar – full of memories and shared laughter, which nurtured and protected me just as the cottage itself did.

In the lead up to the move I was fearful of the unknown since my coping mechanism to date had hinged entirely on feeling safe. I was sensitive to the fact that I was moving into a house where there were no patterns of daily life, no sense of me or us and how we had lived. My strategy was to set myself four weeks to put enough of myself on the design of the cottage prior to moving in, to make it feel familiar from the moment I crossed the threshold.

What makes the layout of the Pheasantry cosy and successful is the fact that it revolves around one welcoming sitting room that stretches the length of the cottage, from where you can open the door onto far-reaching views, as well as curl up with fires lit at either end. A winding staircase leads up to a small landing from which open three bedrooms and a long room, which evolved into a work space over time.

following pages
The Pheasantry, a
19th-century cottage
nestled in the woods, with
its small and perfectly
formed façade, and my
growing collection of pots
– blooming acidanthera,
salvias and pelargoniums
– the start of another
rambling collection.

There is a small bathroom that, largely thanks to the view of the oak tree from the claw-footed bath, is one of my favourite rooms of all time. Watching spring arrive with shoots of green on that tree gave me a conscious realisation of new life emerging.

Everything about the way that I decorated the cottage played a part in holding me up. Whether it was the soft old-fashioned wisteria wallpaper that I hung in my bedroom, which immediately felt like an old friend, or a pair of crewelwork curtains I'd bought years before for the sense of belonging that they would bring to a room: piece by piece I built a protective and strengthening world around myself.

In the same vein, my things carried vast depths of meaning, even more than before. In the same way as journalling helps many, unpacking and arranging the things that I loved and cherished helped me to regain my sense of self. The stones that we collected on the beach from holidays in the Jura together littered my window sills. The portrait of our beloved spaniel, Humbug, that I had given Ant for Christmas hung facing my bed. The photographs from his mantelpiece now sat on mine. The placement of these things was ritualistic and the process was soulful. I was particular in the extreme about arranging it just so, even by my own standards. But creating this home was something that gave me a sense of control and my own agency. It was a place where I had choices again and could hold on enough to let go.

Though it wasn't always easy to fulfil the more creative demands of my job at a time when I felt so depleted, in retrospect, my work saved me. I was fortunate to still have the loyal support of both my clients and colleagues who held my hand as they encouraged me to fulfil the projects I was working on. My home life was still quiet, and the pace was slow. I was finding a way to live that softened the hard edge of reality.

Looking back, the home where my One Day Box came into its own was a place where it took on life-saving properties, building me up and pulling me back onto my feet. Living at the cottage was a new chapter for me and a cathartic one.

The dining room end of this double-aspect room has a handsome oak centre table with a brass-studded pedestal base. The more delicate dining chairs are covered in a modern purple weave with leather piping and a contemporary French hanging light is above.

Contemporary faience plates and a landscape that echoes the hills overlooking the cottage sit above the mantel. A large early-20th-century Fortuny screen was bought for a project, but I could not resist cutting it in half to flank (to the millimetre) the chimney breast, giving another layer of patina in an otherwise painted room.

My love of collecting still lifes started around the time I bought this cyclamen oil painting – a plant that always reminds me of my grandmother.

The sitting room is all about comfort and has always been an inviting space. Treasured paintings cover the walls, including a favourite modern Scottish colourist landscape given to me, and a much-loved Suzani hangs off the back of a generous Howard sofa.

Antique crewel curtains with an old leather and silk flat braid that I love frame the garden door and upstairs landing sash window, while moss-coloured wool curtains hang on the other three windows in this room.

The Prince of Wales feather-adorned mirror sits on a marbleised painted slate mantel, with a revolving display of favourite photographs and cards. Bookcases echoing the opposite alcoves are filled with my most loved books.

above

Anglepoise shell lights frame this window and often dog-strewn sofa, where there is little room for table lamps. A blooming pelargonium fills the window and a Chartwell Weave ottoman is covered with more books and magazines.

right

A worn cushion made for my grand-mother by the National Theatre costume department, with whom she worked for many years while chairman there in the 1990s, sits on her old rose-covered sofa.

left
In this compact and filled entrance
hall, deep grenache walls show off the
hint of gilt on the leaf lantern. Well-
used riding coats and boots, and my
gaudy market bag – a nod to Dama –
line the walls and welcome you as you
step over the threshold of the back
door to the cottage.

above
This cosy kitchen is dominated
by a Swedish refectory table and a
set of Arts and Crafts chairs. The
needlework bull has followed me
around from kitchen to kitchen,
as have the cookbooks. The pine
cupboards were repainted in indigo
blue and Cornucopia is on the
roman blinds.

following pages
The gilded starburst clock inherited
from Grandmama hangs behind
a French ceramic lamp, with a
lampshade made from an old floral
linen fragment and a photograph of
my parents on their wedding day.
The fruits of my newly planted
cutting garden jostle for attention in
Lustreware on this sofa table.

left

The wisteria wallpaper sets the tone of a nostalgic, feminine and enveloping bedroom, with treasured objects at every turn. A voile backdrop to the bed, alongside cream Belgian linen curtains, are kept simple due to the scale of the room. Humbug and Coco assume their usual position on the antique French bedspread.

above

An archived lilac print hangs above the claw-footed bath. Above the sink is a shell mirror made in Norfolk, and collected Mochaware sits on the shelf with other chipped china teacups. Stones collected from beach walks litter the windowsill with gilt-edged glass decanters.

above

The large-scale mirror opens up this room, bouncing light into the corridor beyond. A favourite patchwork bedspread and antique Tibetan rug layer this soft pink guest bedroom, with an old-fashioned floral linen on the curtains and a paisley shade perched on a coral wicker lamp.

right

The view from the landing to my bedroom, with Oulton Stripe on this ordinarily clothes-strewn armchair. Every object tells a story, including the battered vintage suitcase I gave to Ant, well-travelled way before his time.

following pages

The inaugural Dahlias bedroom is chaotic, exuberant and joyful. A motley selection of needlework and ikat cushions sit on a red bedspread and a ruby glass lamp has a vivid yellow silk lampshade.

previous pages
Simple red and white woven curtains, a
Honeycomb saffron coloured nursing
chair and a sari ruched lampshade
all offset this blousy wallpaper. It
is testament to my 'more is more'
approach to colour, pattern and
decorating.

previous pages, continued
Cosmos picked from the garden spills
out of an antique indigo glass jug on
the landing. A small ebonised chair,
upholstered in drap de soie, sits on a
contemporary Indian flat weave dhurrie.
Textiles collected are framed and
hanging over the bannisters.

following pages
At the Pheasantry, planting and tending
to a garden felt like a lifeline to me. With
the help of an extraordinary plantsman
and gardener, Robert, we poured much
love and time into these abundant borders
alongside the swimming pool which I
fashioned into an ornamental pond.

CHAPTER FOUR

From Refuge to New Energy

I WAS, AND WILL ALWAYS REMAIN, AWARE OF how enormously lucky I was to have the opportunity to live somewhere like the Pheasantry. Being surrounded by the woods was not only reassuring, it was inspiring too. Added to which, I had space and time on my hands. I was drawn back to my archive of fabrics, which by now had long grown out of one box and into many trunks, scattered between my office, my old home and the garage of my cottage. It felt like the right time to bring them all together in one place and doing this became a catalyst for creativity and productivity.

It felt like a natural transition to translate the extent of my collecting into something more tangible. I wanted to explore an expression of myself beyond the interiors projects I worked on for my clients. With Ant's encouraging words echoing in my ears, rifling through my One Day Box in this way felt purposeful and authentic. The idea of some of these designs coming to life had been at the back of my mind for a long time. In taking this step forward, I was playing an active role in writing the next chapter of my life, and it felt great.

forging ahead

previous pages
The long room that
became my workroom
was at the back of
the cottage. A purple
moleskin felt French
armchair sits with a
view of the woods, onto
which Humbug looks.
A wallpapered Dahlias
screen breaks up the
space and the floor and
tabletops are covered
in samples of the new
collection, trials of
products being made
and designs in progress.

In a design world where there was so much already on offer of real value and interest, I focused on how best to translate the story of these collected items. I was inherently aware that the origins and story of each fragment I was reinterpreting needed to be told. Looking back at my childhood influences, it's hardly surprising that the designs I champion and the aesthetic I am drawn to are from a bygone era. There is a richness, an over-the-top-ness and a depth that give full rein to my diehard belief that less is never more. Timelessness is my Holy Grail.

Keen to understand and maintain the key ingredients of these designs, both in where they originated from as well as in how they were made, I looked to British craftsmanship as the channel through which to achieve this. In doing so, I accessed a world of traditional and technical mastery.

I forged new friendships and was introduced to some of the best makers for the task of bringing my designs to life. I have a pretty clear vision of colour and texture, or at least I know what I like, but I was an amateur and I am hugely grateful to the specialists who shared their knowledge so generously. I found myself immersed in an inspiring community who opened up their own archives for me to learn from. Their enthusiasm engulfed me, and it was exhilarating.

The process involved much to-ing and fro-ing, for which, because it was dependent on complex traditional techniques, there were no short cuts. In those early stages my focus was not a commercial one, so there was a freedom in the way the designs emerged. Gradually, as production gained momentum, I was hungry to share it all with a wider audience.

In June 2019 I launched six designs five miles down the road from my home in Dorset. The backdrop was a deconstructed barn belonging to a talented dealer and friend of mine, Edward Hurst. It is a wonderfully pared-back space, lovingly restored by him and littered with his exquisite things. People I'd admired in the industry for so long travelled to see my new wares and I was bowled over by everyone's generosity, enthusiasm and support.

opposite
Early cuttings of the
Dahlias hand block-
printed wallpaper being
sampled alongside
fragments of damask,
a coveted Italian
cut-velvet cushion and
striped wallpapers that
are waiting in the wings
all gather on my kilim-
topped workbench at
the Pheasantry. A large
needlework cushion of
pomegranates sits as a
reminder of jewel tones.

previous pages
The romanticism of this George III
four-poster bed with original iris
embroidered hangings, alongside
Enid's Garland, with overlapping
dog rose branches, underlines the
whimsical vision I had envisaged.

left and following pages
The Dahlias hand block-printed
wallpaper serve as a dramatic
backdrop to this exquisite
18th-century Italian side table and
17th-century Louis XIV table clock.

Dahlias wallpaper provides a
backdrop for a George III wheelback
embroidered side chair, and Enid's
Garland to an 18th-century painted
elbow chair respectively.

above
Edward Hurst's beautifully restored
mid-19th-century brick and flint
barn was the perfect place to launch
my collection.

previous pages and right
Jane Hurst helped with
the extraordinary array
of early summer flowers
for the launch of the
collection. A horsebox
was strewn with Enid's
Garland and transformed
into a bar. Displays of
delphiniums, lupins,
scabious, peonies, phlox
and clematis, among many
others, were abundant.

Long refectory
tables were covered
with our Cornucopia
tablecloths and lined with
Honeycomb-covered
chairs in all colours.
The overall effect was
a glimpse into the
chaos and colour of my
collecting habit.

A family of friends

left
Four-legged friends
feature heavily in
my life. My beloved
horse Fina was the
perfect model for
the launch of the
Pavilion Collection.

I didn't plan with a coherent collection in mind, but once I had chosen the final six designs, they spoke to each other as friends. I like to imagine that if they were sitting around a table, conversation would be free-flowing. As I write, I am working on my fifth collection. Though the range of designs and products has expanded, with new characters bringing their voices to the table all the time, that very first collection remains a true and lasting statement of intent.

While my style will always champion maximalism, there are endless new avenues to explore. From a specific method of printing that I adopted in my first collection to a new technique of weaving I've implemented more recently, every day of research uncovers unexpected finds. My hope is that my reinterpretation of the designs I love will do justice to the originals that started this journey – and that the conversations they help to generate in the rooms where they are used are as lively in people's homes as they are in my imagination.

below
Enid, Dilys and Stanley
make themselves at
home on a Honeycomb
sofa with Enid's
namesake floral print
'Enid's Garland' on the
curtains framing the
windows beyond.

The Pavilion Collection

The Pavilion Collection is a family of stripes. Inspired by some 1920s
samplers I cherished, there is something about the breadth of that
stripe and freshness of these colours employed in this design (with
that unlikely lilac) that conjure up the glamour of a Slim Aarons
photograph. It prompted our first foray into outdoor fabrics, making
this jewel-like striped world as happy inside as out.

Chartwell Weave

Chartwell Weave is inspired by
a Scottish bridge cloth that was,
in hindsight, far too ambitious as
my first foray into the world of
weaving. It was a labour of love:
I wasn't willing to compromise on
the intricacies of this pattern and
the depth that I wanted to achieve.
It owes its name to my great-
grandparents' house and the Arts
and Crafts style I love.

Serafina

Less of a hero and more of a staple, the Serafina Weave is a go-to
fabric to bind things together. Once again, I couldn't resist the full
gambit of colours that could be achieved, making it the perfect friend
to the rest of the collection.

Walsingham Weave

My take on that irresistible flame-stitch pattern, this was inspired
by a postage stamp-sized fragment I pocketed years ago. It's a
heavyweight cloth which packs as much of a punch on its designed
face-side as it does on its reverse. It adds weight, personality and
patina and I find myself turning to it again and again.

Honeycomb

For a relatively simple design, Honeycomb was drawn out of a remarkably opulent damask. I found the process of stripping it back deeply rewarding – moving from the starting point of a large-scale pattern, to a more subtle weave. Dressed up or dressed down, this was one of my first designs and remains a favourite.

Chequerboard Stitch

Broadening our collection of weaves, this relatively vibrant and
sumptuous fabric became the more dominant force alongside its more
subdued sister Serafina. It's the type of design I naturally gravitate
towards, and works brilliantly with many of the prints and weaves in
the collection.

Oulton Stripe

Named after the village where Ant and I lived in North Norfolk, Oulton Stripe harnesses the inner magpie in me. Inspired by a well-travelled Syrian blanket, I was particularly drawn to a specific thread of gold that I wanted to reproduce. I chose four colourways, each of which has an otherworldly quality that I love.

Cornucopia

Cornucopia is decadent, theatrical and slightly clumsy. It was the
first fragment that sprung out at me from my trunk on a crude
hessian, almost hand-painted, cloth which I'd bought in a market
in France. Steeped in tradition, with a tree of life quality, it takes
centre stage in any room in which it is used.

Enid's Garland

Enid's Garland derived from some floral linen sheets that I had for
years. There's a Bloomsbury spirit to its whimsical trailing vine, and
a not-quite-rightness to the coral, lilac and indigo blue, which flourish
alongside each other. It is quirky and joyful and named after my
beloved Dachshund, Enid.

Enid's Ramble

This is a simplified adaptation of my much-loved Enid's Garland, the
artwork was already in place but the 'more is more' result that comes
with producing it on a smaller-scale makes it a modern-day Toile de
Jouy that I just could not resist.

Dahlias

The least commercial design imaginable, the Dahlias originated from
a fragment I fell in love with at first sight. Re-creating that painterly
quality could only be achieved by traditional methods. It was a
signature print I was proud to put my name to as a wallpaper, and
soon after was replicated as a printed linen.

Gilded Rope

This was inspired by the first roll of antique wallpaper I ever bought, making it destined to join my repertoire. Its handsome design hinges on the quality of that smoldering gold and chalky paper, which sets a sultry scene.

6.6m
1.4m

COLOUR:
FAUNA   CHICK
DATE REC'D: 21-2-18
PIECE N°.:   40161
LOT N°:   AK
14.8m

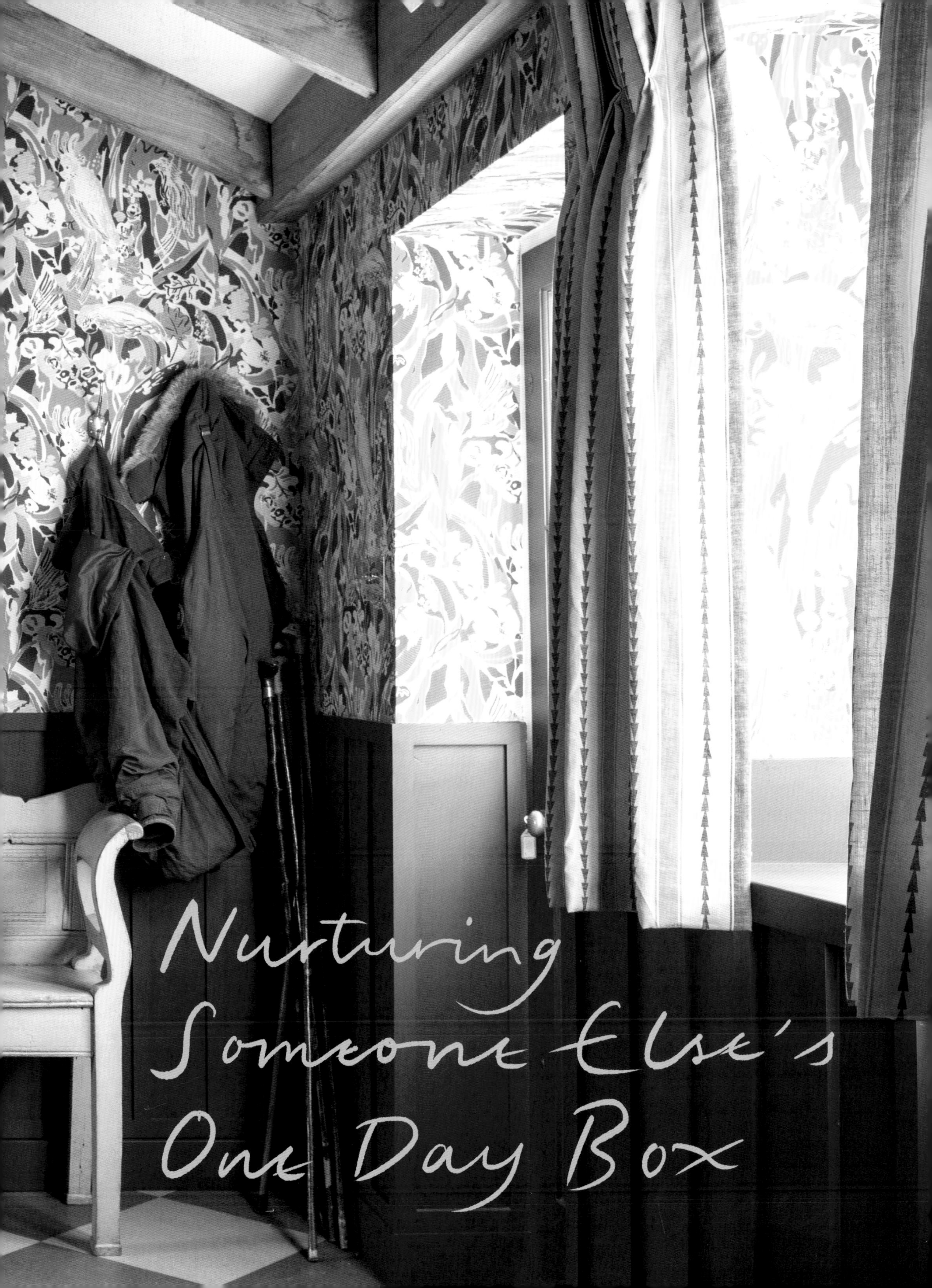

CHAPTER FIVE

Nurturing
Someone Else's
One Day Box

I AM AN INTERIOR DESIGNER: I HELP PEOPLE to design homes that support and inspire their lives. On paper, it's a simple premise: pick up the house and turn it upside down, and everything that moves falls under my remit. In reality, though, it involves much more than that. At its heart, it's about building a relationship as we get to know and understand each other better. It is as far away from colouring in by numbers as you can get, and the greatest pleasure imaginable for me to work with people on something so integral to the way they live.

Exploring someone else's One Day Box is an infinitely interesting process — whether theirs is metaphorical or literal, whether at the beginning, middle or end of its incarnation, or whether they are only tapping in to it now. We all have associations, for whatever reason, with things that make us feel uplifted and held. Some clients come with a houseful of belongings, others with a blank canvas. My aim is to understand with them what sparks memory and brings happiness.

Change is often the catalyst for someone seeking my help. Birth, marriage, moving house, moving country, separating, coming together, and so it goes on. Of course, change is unsettling and, when coupled with the anxiety of making what can be big and costly decisions, it can easily develop into an intimidating experience. But there is an energy that comes with the new that I am drawn to as much for myself as I am when designing for others. As with everything, it's about finding the balance between change and continuity — a nuanced and sometimes complicated, but deeply rewarding process.

previous page
A heavy Voysey-style needlework panel is adapted to upholster this claw-and-ball-footed wing chair, with dyed saffron French linen sheets for its outback, in this majestic hallway.

right
This sitting room gave me an opportunity to curate a more streamlined, clean, colour-filled interior in this London Victorian villa. With handmade cabinetry, a contemporary Italian sofa, mid-century Milo Baughman chairs and a commissioned Indian flatweave dhurrie, everything was bespoke and tailormade.

following pages
Details of a long-standing restoration project in the North of England. This architecturally prominent Palladian house champions craftsmanship and collecting through the decades. The Florentine cassone, with its intricate panels by Lo Scheggia, is used for serving drinks, with 18th-century tapestries hanging the circumference of this oval hall. What was originally the main entrance to the house has become a library, with the elegant 1950s silk curtains serving as the backdrop for an upright reproduction velvet camel-back sofa and contemporary ottoman. The rush matting gives that much-needed added layer of a more organic texture. It is both sumptuous and comfortable, representative of the evolution of this house and its character over time.

previous pages and right
This London town house
was all about colour and
print. As a relatively
compact space, with
the double demand of a
house for both family and
entertaining, meant we
had to be very specific
with the furniture size and
its use. A bespoke shaped
velvet sofa, Danish
mid-century chairs and
a fender create seating
'in the round' as well as
a commissioned folding
drinks table. Grasscloth
walls, blue high gloss
bookcases and a Prussian
blue lacquered dining
room beyond provide a
weighty backdrop for a
wonderfully dynamic art
collection.

following pages
Another city renovation,
this jewel-box study
with bespoke high-gloss
cabinetry doubles as
a working office and
occasional bar. Distinctive
prints favoured by the
client prompted this
very specific hue of red
to be mixed with just
enough blue. Our Semley
armchair in Broken
Stripe ruby is upright but
inviting behind this more
formal desk.

A story of change

left
What could be an imposing space is made less formal by an attractive sofa with a vibrant contemporary bargello weave, off-setting the original wine-red velvet where it could be retained. A sensational 19th-century Karabagh carpet leads through to Cornucopia saffron and indigo curtains, framing the French doors onto the terrace from the dining room beyond.

The lurcher painting, sourced at auction years before, has followed the client's changes of home throughout the years. Giant tree pelargoniums in large-scale antique French ceramic urns breathe life into the space.

I have worked with many clients over long periods of time – updating and evolving their homes as life moves forward, as well as completely redesigning them when they start afresh. This project, a country home in the Cotswolds, was somewhere between the two. The client, Clemmie, had memories of the house as a child because it had belonged to her father. Though it was familiar, it had never been her home, and in moving there from London with her husband and their four children, re-designing the house marked the start of a new life for them, and for the house itself.

The house is eighteenth-century in style, classically designed by the architect Quinlan Terry in the early 1970s, with signature interiors by Sibyl Colefax and John Fowler. The original brief would have been to create a space that focused on formal entertaining, without the need to incorporate the chaos and paraphernalia that comes with many young children. The kitchen was small and barely used, and the rooms were upright and exacting.

In contrast to the previous generation, Clemmie's life follows the beat of a different rhythm. She embraces the comings and goings of family life in a relaxed and informal way, with a caravan of pets following behind. Children, dogs, chickens, horses, geese and a donkey: their home life is vivid and colourful. The first and fundamental step for me was to make the space work specifically for this incoming young family, while simultaneously appreciating the history of the house.

Having been lucky enough to work with the family on their previous home in London, and knowing Clemmie well, I understood the patterns of their life, the personalities involved and what did and didn't matter to each of them.

In the middle of the house is a sweeping Gone-With-The-Wind-style staircase, which easily assumes the central focus. But its formality didn't fit with the family's way of being. So instead, while keeping some of the original artwork from before, we included others alongside that the family had collected and loved, and in doing so changed the conversation. Toned down and informal, the welcome is much warmer.

following pages
This kitchen was a collaboration between myself and Jane Taylor, a truly original architectural designer and friend. Streamlined and practical, while being suitably robust and elegant, the design was focused on creating a working space for an enthusiastic cook. Focusing on this dynamic landscape etching, we framed the robust aga and artwork with elongated shelves housing collected detritus, pots and pans, with brass fittings aplenty.

above

The sitting room is at the end of the family kitchen (pictured opposite) and underlines the informality of how this space is used. Old and new textiles – our Chartwell Weave ottoman, antique-fragment cushions, and a more muted Ghiordes early-20th-century carpet – intermingle.

The main priority for these clients was the kitchen, now the heart of the house. We knocked three rooms together and light now pours in from sash windows on every side. The layout is streamlined but the design is luxurious and decadent in colour, with an aga at its heart that is constantly humming. We repurposed much of the family's furniture, reupholstering it in an array of jewel-toned fabrics. Sofas and armchairs for children and dogs abound. The amalgamation of both our eyes on this room felt natural and decisions were easy to make.

Clemmie has a distinctive style and is not afraid to try something new, giving me free reign to unleash the unorthodox on an otherwise

above
The contrast of bold
elements with the more
traditional architecture
of a country house was
the defining principle of
this room. A bold brass
lantern and bespoke Italian
lacquer fridge sit alongside
the more delicate Enid's
Garland curtains that frame
the windows throughout.

ordinary space. The boot room, which had previously been an indus-
trial kitchen, now has tropical wallpaper, a citrus-yellow antique bench
(relinquished from my One Day Box), an irregular patterned lino floor,
bespoke green cupboards and a cobalt baize door, all an expression of
the family's eclectic personality.

The dining room was an awkward railway-carriage-type room, only
used on high days and holidays. Our approach was to convert it into a
jewel box, a space that feels luxurious – lacquered in saffron yellow and
complemented by my Cornucopia curtains, alongside the striking Gary
Hume figurative works lining the walls.

following pages
Nothing takes itself too
seriously in this boot
room. An unexpected
wallpaper sets the tone
with a Swedish-inspired
lino tiled floor, cupboards
full of muddy boots,
slate-topped units and a
vivid blue baize swing
door lead through to the
laundry room beyond.

left

This connecting annexe
originally led through to
some stables, which have
since been converted
into a pool house. The
climbing wallpaper, our
Plain Stripe in emerald,
and a series of modern
verdigris lanterns lead
to a vibrant yellow
changing room. The
focus on bringing the
outside in is paramount
in this connecting space
between the garden
via the French doors,
the pool area and the
main house.

right

The least-altered room
in the house, the sitting
room still upholds
it original Colefax
foundation decor. The
tobacco-coloured walls
were updated to a
softer blue-grey, but the
furniture and paintings
remain. Inherited
upholstery in its richer
tones is accompanied by
a fresh floral linen and
antique chintz cushions.
A tailored contempo-
rary tartan ottoman,
midnight-blue horsehair
fender and an uplifting
early-20th-century
Sultanabad carpet tie
this more formal space
together with a sense
of ease.

left and above
The client's own stamp
is all over this room.
Large windows have been
overhauled with Dahlias
linen. Fabric lined walls
create a cocoon-like
space, with a lofty tester
and our Walsingham
Weave used in reverse
to ground this otherwise
feminine bedroom. Enid's
Ramble wallpaper lines
the walls of the bathroom,
and amassed artwork
and textiles, Dahlias and
Enid's Ramble lawn linen,
make this space layered
and inviting.

Much like how I would approach my own home, it was important to Clemmie that their bedroom had soul. Dahlias was the ideal expression of her flamboyant style and sets the tone for a series of rooms as soon as you walk in. A mammoth bed and huge patchwork quilt are more often than not covered in languishing teenagers and dogs. Opulent and spoiling but unrestrained and un-precious – this bedroom, bathroom and adjoining dressing room were a joy to design.

Everything about the way the house is decorated now lends itself as much to the bustle of everyday life, as it does to entertaining on a larger scale. Seemingly practical spaces don't have to be inferior and every room has a quiet confidence. It is a fun, welcoming and inspiring place to be and, just like Clemmie and her family, there is nothing too uptight or over-designed about it.

following pages
The dressing room is
testament to my client's
passion for colour. Our
Dahlias wallpaper and
ruched blind offset
the graphic rug not to
mention her wonderfully
colourful wardrobe.

The girls' attic bedroom
is lined in an old-
fashioned strawberries
wallpaper with matching
Scottish antique blankets
on each bed.

CHAPTER SIX

Looking Forward,
Looking Back

For all the time, thought and obsessing I've put into being the architect of my future, I should know by now that's not how it plays out. After the launch, my life was filled with interiors projects, and the early days of the collection were busy. I was taking one step at a time and I could never have envisaged how my life was about to change in the most joyous and spectacular way. That's when I bumped into Blondie at the local village shop.

The next chapter

Blondie's handmade large-scale ceramic twisted sculpture 'Energy', in a Barium blue glaze, sits dynamically in the woods behind our house.

Typically, I was rooting around with boxes in the back of my car when we waved to each other. We'd met a few years before, but we hadn't seen each other since. We were both rebuilding our lives in ways that were new to us and there was an immediate and irresistible connection. This seismic shift in our shared state of happiness, and frankly pinch-me disbelief, meant that life turned on its axis and became about opportunity and hope again.

Blondie is a ceramic artist, and a hugely talented one. While the media we use are different, we come together in our shared love of beautiful things. The irony is that inherently Blondie is a minimalist. The fruits of his talent are the result of the exacting perfectionism of his craft. He has worn the same navy sweatshirt to his studio for fourteen years on the trot, he travels light, often with only a plastic bag. But he has bought into my cluttered way of living with an open heart and mind. Whether it's the beautiful pink rose he gave me for my garden on an early date, the antique glass vase that sits by my bed or his monumental glazed pots that now frame our front door, he participates enthusiastically in my passion for collecting in all its mad glory.

The greatest gift Blondie has given me has been our daughter, Lily Hope, born in April 2020. We revelled in her arrival and we haven't stopped since. Together with Lily and my stepchildren, Pom and Jacobi, I find myself at the centre of a bustling and full-hearted family of five, complete with spaniels, budgies, bantams and bunnies. It is hectic, noisy and glorious.

Piecing together our home through the eyes of our daughter has brought back to mind so many elements of my childhood that I'd carefully stored away in my One Day Box. It gives me great pleasure to see the carved angels above her bed that once sat above mine, and even more to have the conversations they spark. I adore the feeling of familiarity my old Molly Brett prints bring to her room, now hung

In 2015 Blondie exhibited
a large body of work at
Chatsworth after a long
career working in the UK
and abroad as a ceramic
artist. These sculptures were
created over a period of three
years, and here he is seen
with a trio of large stone-
ware glazed vessels named
'Contemplation'. His work-
shop is near our home in
Dorset, where he continues
to develop ambitious and
large-scale works.

alongside a Henry Lamb drawing given to her by a beloved neighbour. Of course, Blondie's story is there too, with a pair of Wemyss pottery pigs collected by him for her bedside table. To complete the picture, the room is looked over by the watchful eye of her sister's oversized fluffy unicorn and many of her brother's well-thumbed story books. Lily's room holds her story alongside all of ours, and in doing so, provides a space to feel safe as she finds her own way.

As I did with my mother, Lily has picked up on the language I use around these belongings. My friends have often mocked my enthusiastic use of adjectives: some 'ravishing' Dahlias, the 'sumptuous' bedroom, a 'sensational' wardrobe. Lily now pulls the black pebble I collected off a Sussex beach on the morning of Ant's funeral out of my bedside table drawer and fondly calls it Mummy's 'precious' stone. I wonder if she'll collect words in the way I've collected things.

Life here is unfolding in a natural way, full of the comings and goings of work, school life and friends. There is a round table in the corner of our kitchen, which opens onto the garden beyond. Nothing makes me happier than when friends, expected or otherwise, drop in from down the lane, the perfect antidote to the fast pace of life. I still feel nostalgic but it's no longer an ache. Looking at our shared mantelpiece charting the colour and chaos of all of our lives, it's not hard to see why.

Lily Hope sits in her father's hand-thrown glazed terracotta pot, surrounded by salvias amassed over time. My passion for dahlias has been, so far, adopted by Lily as a love for jewel colours, if nothing else.

right

The mantelpiece in
our kitchen houses the
relocated overmantel
mirror from the
Pheasantry. Collected old
and new ceramics, paper
tulips in Blondie's smaller
edition vases, remnant
balloons from a birthday
party, photographs of
loved ones and a scalloped
needlework line this ever-
changing mantel.

following pages

Much to his horror,
Blondie's bookcases have
been transformed from
pillar box red to a more
matte blue-black, housing
our collected library of art
and design books. An old
Howard shaped sofa has
been revived in my most
favourite French cotton
chintz, heaving with
Plain Stripe, Walsingham
Weave, and wonderfully
dog-eared cushions. This
study room where we
gather to watch television
is colourful and deeply
comfortable.

left
Coco lies on a Plain Stripe ruby upholstered sofa. An early Ikat cushion collected many years prior hangs on for dear life, while flame-stitch needlework panels have been converted into heavy cushions. A vast and sublime example of an early Kente cloth hangs over the back.

following pages
An antique etched French lamp sits on top of a gilded masked marble-topped console table. As is my wont when wall space is running out, a photograph of Clementine Churchill leans against the wall, alongside a landscape teetering on the edge. Antique glassware sits alongside dahlias from the garden.

Humbug dozes on our Dahlias-covered Barsham Sofa surrounded by Oulton Stripe cushions and a needlework find from a car boot sale. Walsingham weave covers a shaped antique ottoman in front of the fire.

…IN TUCKER SMITH, SONS OF JOHN SMITH OF DALE PARK, SUSSEX

right

A large-scale Regency Gothic oak table sits in our entrance hall, laden with what might be deemed clutter by some, but represents cherished memories to us: early smiles snapped with my stepchildren, my siblings and me, Blondie with his little girl and Ant smiling down from the gilded mirror above. Dahlias lampshades sit proud on top of bronze column lamps, one adorned with a dog rosette won at the local village fete.

following pages

Dinner at our winter wedding, where the tent was transformed with greenery foraged from our home in Dorset, as well the hedgerows in Norfolk. More was certainly more with the ravishing flowers executed in collaboration between Tattie Rose Studio and myself. A vast mirrored disco ball and ruched gold lamé panels framed a magical evening with friends and family, heaving with happiness.

Coming together

Lily Hope as a toddler, climbing on our childhood pram covered in Plain Stripe in emerald, accompanied by Clover the Shetland pony – all sitting underneath a horse chestnut tree in full bloom.

Every time I return to Norfolk, the place where this story began, I feel it is a celebration. Home is still the heart of our family, and its magnetic pull remains strong in our lives. Together with my sister, brother and all of our children, we continue to relive and celebrate the patterns of our own childhoods. We are keenly aware of how immensely privileged we are to have had the security and enjoyment of this home as the backbone of our lives, and of the continued responsibility that this carries.

Gathering there today is about the next generation coming together and nurturing that feeling of belonging to this place. What was a treehouse has become a bell tent, the working Suffolk Punch is now a red tractor and the swing seat that overlooked my grandmother's bed of dahlias has been reimagined. The adventures they still inspire, however, are just as memorable.

There are touchstones that remain unchanged. The rocking horse still squeaks in the hallway, the pram goes under the same tree and the next generation of greedy ponies, smelling just like their predecessors, nudge their way into our children's lives.

Recently I redecorated the down-at-heel but much-loved bedroom that had been mine as a child. I know every single centimetre of that room intimately. The wallpaper and fabrics I used from my own collection echo the style of both of my grandmothers, as well as carrying my memories of that room as a girl – midnight feasts I laid out on the floor and the books I read in that same chair. The floral patterns, slightly jarring colours and whiff of over-the-topness are a nod to the people who shaped me and the time spent in this house. I slept there the night before our wedding, Lily holds her own tea parties on the rug, and the dogs always find their way to the end of the bed as soon as we arrive. New memories are being made and enjoyed, and the story rolls on.

There's no right way of living, there's no right way of decorating: we are all feeling our way. Homes change as our circumstances change

The entrance hallway to my parents' home is lined with oak coffers and an Edwardian rocking horse. Specialist painted stone block walls and a faux vaulted ceiling create a more theatrical but welcoming entrance, flanked by tole wall lanterns, to the hall beyond.

in the ebb and flow of life. These projects are a constant and rewarding labour of love: reimagining spaces, rearranging furniture, finding fresh ways to create interiors that are aligned with what matters. And there, for me, lie both the challenge and the deep fulfilment.

However much I pore over detail, what really matters is the living of life. Home ultimately is the people – past and present – who have held, supported and inspired me the most, and they are the ones I am honouring in this process. That's most celebrated when we come together around a table, piling in with stories and delicious food, children, family and friends. I thank them for humouring my One Day Box tendencies which, to the surprise of all of us, have ended up being the route to so much that I have to be grateful for.

Finally, an ode to that box. Not unlike Mary Poppins's bottomless carpet-bag in its seemingly endless supply of random beauties, it has carried and inspired so much adventure, helping me through sometimes painful, often exhilarating and always heartfelt experiences along the way.

left and following pages
This bedroom
wallpapered in Enid's
Ramble plum is given a
brief moment's respite
with the gentle floral voile
bed tester. A cacophony
of Enid's Garland
otherwise adorns the
headboard, valance,
curtains and armchair
in this room. A fuchsia-
covered serpentine end
sofa sits at the foot of
the bed, covered by an
antique crochet bedspread
and the inevitable dogs.

Assorted collected
plates and prints hang on
the walls, telling the story
of this room from it being
my mother's childhood
bedroom, to mine.
Well-thumbed Beatrix
Potter books rest on the
mantelpiece beneath
a colourful still life of
tulips. An occasional table
is haphazardly covered
with a vintage linen and
lace cloth.

THE TALE OF Mr. JEREMY FISHER
THE TALE OF Mrs. TIGGY-WINKLE
THE TALE OF Mr. JEREMY FISHER
THE TALE OF SQUIR
THE TALE OF PIGLING BLAND
THE TALE OF MRS TITTLEMOUSE
THE TALE OF JEMIMA PUDDLE-DUCK
THE TALE OF JOHNNY TOWN-MOUSE
THE TALE OF Mrs. TIGGY-WINKLE
THE TALE OF Mrs. TITTLEMOUSE

The Tale of MR. JEREMY FISHER

The Tale of JEMIMA PUDDLE-DUCK

The Tale of MR. JEREMY FISHER

The Tale of Mrs. TITTLEMOUSE

The Tale of TOM KITTEN

left
A bathroom is given shape with a theatrical opening for the Edwardian bath lined in Dahlias wallpaper and framed by old spot voile curtains – a later addition alongside the gilt pair of candelabra. A Dahlias Maud slipper chair and ruched blinds gild the lily.

above
The accompanying loo, with matching wallpaper, has a reused toile curtain.

following pages
Ebonised bookcases are tucked into the corners of this decadent adjoining space, where china sits on every surface, with the Lustreware again making an appearance.

left
This parrot-strewn
linen sofa in soft muted
colours gives way to the
otherwise richer and more
dominant furniture. The
decorative urn lamps were
the starting point for the
colours in this drawing
room. The light pours in
from the conservatory
beyond, providing a
warm and hidden spot to
seek refuge in an always
humming house.

following pages
Picnics on top of the hill
overlooking the house,
with rugs, drinks and
sometimes horses too, are
the highlight of summers
spent in Norfolk.

My mother with her
beloved horse Winston,
Lily Hope, myself and my
sister with her boys gather
in the long grass.

previous page
Bamboo loungers sit
by the pool where this
corner is sheltered by
towering grasses and
cardoons, in this Gertrude
Jekyll-planted yew
walled garden.

left
My grandparents' old
swing seat has been
restored with Plain Stripe
ruby on the cushions and
canopy, dotted and lined
in Enid's Ramble cush-
ions; it is a magical spot.

following pages
Summer days at home:
children and dogs play in
the garden, while a bar is
set up on a stone pedestal
in the glasshouse leading
on to a lakeside supper
beyond.

Acknowledgements

Thank you…

To my husband, Blondie: I owe so much to you both as an artist and as supporter-in-chief – you have inspired me every step of the way. Since we met, and subsequently throughout the writing of this book, you haven't just kept me sane, you've made me happier than I thought possible. Thank you, from the bottom of my heart, for everything, especially your calm understanding… dare I say appreciation… of my bonkers collecting habit, and for even letting me keep Enid's whiskers on our mantelpiece.

To Lily Hope, for lighting up my every day – I hope when you've grown up, you'll forgive me for my inclusion of so many photographs of you. Such happy days together.

To my stepchildren, Pom Pom and Jacobi – for always bringing your love and laughter wherever we go, and to all those integrally involved in our home life, who've been swept along in the tidal wave that has been this book.

To my sister, Gemma – I can't put into words how much I have to be grateful to you for. Your way with words is just the start.

To my family, who have supported me wholeheartedly and helped me in so many ways: my parents, my brother Archie, my uncles and aunts and Nonie Chapman. Thank you for sharing your memories and photograph albums so generously and entrusting me to capture some of those precious moments in this book.

To Christianne, thank you for being an extraordinary support and objective ear and eye throughout this whole process. Your expertise in helping others to be understood and, importantly, heard, is rare and true – and I am forever in debt for your holding my hand through the writing of this very personal account.

To the team who've worked with me over the years and today, Philippa, Anna, Venetia, Phoebe, Stella, Octavia, Lucy, Laura, Issy, Max, George, Mary and Georgie. You've made the curve balls an adventure rather than a disaster, and I'm so grateful for your commitment, care and kindness. And to my sounding boards for so much, Katharine Howard and Flora Astor. I couldn't ask for more.

To all the talented makers I've had (and continue to have) the privilege to work with, for opening my eyes to the true beauty of craftsmanship. Thank you for your patience and your creativity – you are a constant source of inspiration to the whole team and we salute you.

To Ken Bolan, the doyen of eclecticism, my first long-standing employer. Thank you for entrusting me with so much and setting the bar, not just in being bold with collecting but brave with decisions in life too.

To Robert Dalrymple, what a privilege to get to know you and to embark on this project together. You have taught me so much, not least the beauty of a less cluttered, kaleidoscopic page. Thank you for your patience with the to-ing and fro-ing, often at a distance, and the elegant way you pointed me in the right direction.

To Alexandra 'Fin' Fellowes, my extremely talented friend, whose exacting eye in graphic design knows no bounds.

To all the brilliantly talented photographers I have worked with over the last twenty years, my dear friends Bill Batten and Simon Upton for your extraordinary work and dedication to the cause – and the teams around you. Natalie, Emma, Tom, Sara and Gabby – I have so enjoyed our long days together and look forward to many more.

To the team at Rizzoli – Charles Miers and Victorine Lamothe – for giving me a go and finding just the right balance of challenge and support to get this extremely personal account (which was never anticipated) over the line. Also, to Maria Pia Gramaglia and Johanna Stephenson for your contribution. And to Laura Burlington for setting the ball rolling.

To my family of friends. You know who you are. Thank you for carrying me through so much with such generosity and good humour. You made the bleakest days possible and the brightest days even better.

Finally, to all my clients and those who so generously allowed me to photograph their houses – thank you for inviting me into your homes with such open hearts and minds.

Flora Soames · The One Day Box

First published in the United States
of America in 2023 by
Rizzoli International Publications, Inc.
300 Park Avenue South
New York, NY 10010

www.rizzoliusa.com

Copyright © 2023 Flora Soames

Art Direction: Flora Soames
Design: Robert Dalrymple

Publisher: Charles Miers
Editor: Victorine Lamothe
Production Manager: Maria Pia Gramaglia
Managing Editor: Lynn Scrabis

*All rights reserved. No part of this publication may be
reproduced, stored in a retrieval system, or transmitted
in any form or by any means, electronic, mechanical,
photocopying, recording, or otherwise, without prior
consent of the publisher.*

Printed in Italy

2023 2024 2025 2026 / 10 9 8 7 6 5 4 3 2 1

ISBN: 978-0-8478-7365-4
Library of Congress Control Number: 2023931588

Visit us online:
Facebook.com/RizzoliNewYork
Twitter: @Rizzoli_Books
Instagram.com/RizzoliBooks
Pinterest.com/RizzoliBooks
Youtube.com/user/RizzoliNY
Issuu.com/Rizzoli

Photographic & Copyright Credits

All photography © Simon Upton
except when noted otherwise.

Pages 44–5 background: © Emma Lewis, remaining images:
© Soames Archive; page 52: © Chris Barham, *Daily Herald*,
Mirrorpix; page 65: © Flora Soames; page 66 bottom left:
© Geoffrey Shakerley Archive; page 67 background:
© Emma Lewis, top and bottom right: © Geoffrey Shakerley
Archive, remaining images © Soames Archive; page 68
© Soames Archive; page 72 bottom left: © Soames Archive,
bottom right: © The Broadwater Collection; page 73
background: © Emma Lewis, remaining images © Soames
Archive; page 74: © Getty Images (UK); page 76: © Reg
Lancaster, *Daily Express*, Mirrorpix; page 77: © Soames
Archive; page 79: © Tim Beddow, *The World of Interiors*,
Condé Nast Publications Ltd; pages 80, 88–96: © Flora
Soames; pages 98–103: © Simon Upton, *House & Garden*,
Condé Nast Publications Ltd; page 104: © Emma Lewis;
pages 105–13: © Simon Upton, *House & Garden*, Condé
Nast Publications Ltd; pages 114–15: © Emma Lewis; pages
116–17: © Simon Upton, *House & Garden*, Condé Nast
Publications Ltd; pages 118–19: © Flora Soames; pages
120–21: © Simon Upton, *House & Garden*, Condé Nast
Publications Ltd; pages 122–23: © Emma Lewis; pages
124–26: © Simon Upton, *House & Garden*, Condé Nast
Publications Ltd; pages 128–39, 141, 150–51: © Emma Lewis;
pages 152–55: © Natalie Dinham; pages 156–57: © Emma
Lewis; pages 158–59: © Natalie Dinham; pages 160–61:
© Emma Lewis; pages 163, 165: © Bill Batten; page 166:
© Natalie Dinham; page 169: © Bill Batten; pages 172–75:
© Natalie Dinham; pages 176–81: © Bill Batten; pages
182–83: © Natalie Dinham; pages 184–87: © Bill Batten;
pages 188–89: © Natalie Dinham; page 190: © Paul Massey,
House & Garden, Condé Nast Publications Ltd; pages 192–97:
© Bill Batten; pages 198–203: © Paul Massey, *House &
Garden*, Condé Nast Publications Ltd; page 206: © Harry
Soames; pages 210–11: © Sean Henry; page 216 middle
left: © Photography by *Inigo*; page 216 remaining images:
© Flora Soames; pages 226–27: © Chris Allerton.